KOREA AT THE CROSSROADS

Implications for American Policy

Founded in 1921, the **Council on Foreign Relations** is an educational institution, a research institution, and a unique forum bringing together leaders from the academic, public, and private worlds. The Council's basic constituency is its members, but it also reaches out to the broader public so as to contribute to the national dialogue on foreign policy. The Council is private and nonpartisan and takes no positions as an organization.

The Council conducts meetings that give its members an opportunity to talk with invited guests from the United States and abroad who have special experience and expertise in international affairs. Its study program explores foreign policy questions through research by the Council's professional staff, visiting Fellows, and others, and through study groups and conferences. The Council also publishes the journal, Foreign Affairs, in addition to books and monographs. It is affiliated with thirty-eight Committees on Foreign Relations located around the country and maintains a Corporation Service Program that provides meetings and other services for its approximately 200 corporate subscribers.

The Asia Society is a nonprofit, nonpartisan public education organization dedicated to increasing American understanding of Asia and its growing importance to the United States and to world relations. Founded in 1956, the Society covers all of Asia—30 countries from Japan to Iran and from Soviet Central Asia to the South Pacific islands. The Contemporary Affairs department of The Asia Society seeks to alert Americans to the key Asian issues of the 1980s, illuminate the policy choices facing decision-makers in the public and private sectors, and strengthen the dialogue between Americans and Asians on the issues and their policy implications. The department identifies issues in consultation with a group of advisers and addresses these issues through studies and publications, national and international conferences, public programs around the U.S., and corporate and media activities.

Responsibility for the facts and opinions expressed in this report rests exclusively with the members of the study mission. The opinions and interpretations expressed in this report do not necessarily represent the views of the Council on Foreign Relations or The Asia Society or their supporters.

For additional information contact:

Council on Foreign Relations
Public Affairs Office
58 East 68th Street
New York, New York 10021

The Asia Society
Contemporary Affairs Department
725 Park Avenue
New York, New York 10021

KOREA
AT THE
CROSSROADS
Implications for American Policy

A Study Group Report

Council on Foreign Relations ◆ The Asia Society

Contents

Foreword

*T*he extraordinary events of summer 1987 have suddenly thrust the Republic of Korea into the consciousness of many Americans. Korea's turn toward a more democratic future, however uncertain that future may be, has helped stimulate a wider awareness of Korea's dynamic economy and society and of its importance to the United States.

The recent developments in South Korea are only part of a complex and still-unfolding process of change which will require informed and flexible American responses in the months and years ahead. Despite the close relationship between Korea and the United States during the past 40 years, the United States will not be able to control future developments in Korea. Whether such influence as we have turns out to be constructive will depend not only on the wisdom of our government, but also on the capacity in the United States for thoughtful public discussion of Korea's historic changes and of U.S.–Korea relations.

This report records the observations and judgments of an American study group on the Republic of Korea (ROK) and U.S.–Korea relations. The study group was organized jointly by the Council on Foreign Relations and The Asia Society at the end of 1986.

The purpose of this study project was to increase American understanding of the Korean situation and to contribute to public debate on U.S. policy among citizens interested broadly in international affairs as well as specialists and policymakers. The sponsors planned that the nonpartisan group would contribute to improved understanding in two ways, first through the publication of this report and, second, by widening the circle of Americans who are interested in and knowledgeable about Korea and who are available to comment publicly and privately on Korean issues.

The Asia Society and the Council on Foreign Relations asked me to chair the study group. We selected as members of the group individuals of distinction from diverse backgrounds and fields who would contribute their experience and judgment to the study, as well as communicate the group's and their personal observations to wider audiences. While most of our members did not begin with a deep knowledge of Korea, the group included members whose expertise in various fields would be helpful to our study.

This study examines a wide range of topics in South Korean politics, economy, security, and international relations. It does not purport, however, to be comprehensive. Rather, it concentrates on the aspects and issues we consider to be most relevant to American understanding of Korea and U.S.–Korea relations, both in the immediate future and in the longer term.

While the division of the Korean peninsula is a major factor for both South Korea and the United States, we have not included North Korean domestic affairs in our study because of the special challenges facing the ROK at this time and the difficulty of obtaining access to information about North Korea.

Our study is based primarily on off-the-record discussions with a large number of Korean and American officials, politicians, scholars, journalists, business executives, social activists and students, and military officers. We sought exposure to contending viewpoints on most issues, and we were indeed fortunate that so many distinguished individuals gave so generously of their time.

Our discussions began in February 1987 with a series of meetings in Washington, D.C. They continued throughout the spring in New York when we met with a number of Koreans invited to share with us their views on Korean politics and the Korean economy. In late May 1987 our group traveled to Korea for five days of meetings with Koreans and Americans. Most of our meetings took place in Seoul, but two of our members traveled for a day to Pusan, Korea's second largest city, to sample opinions there. We were able to see almost all the Koreans we wished to see except President Chun Doo Hwan. Despite our objections, we were not permitted to see opposition leader Kim Dae Jung who was then under house arrest (although some of us were able to meet with him when we returned to Korea in September 1987).

In June we met again in New York to discuss U.S. policy toward Korea and the shape of our report, which we then planned to publish in September 1987. We also requested a meeting with the Permanent Observer of the Democratic People's Republic of Korea (North Korea) to the United Nations in New York to obtain North Korean views on key topics, but our request was denied.

By the time of what we thought would be our last meeting in June, however, dramatic events in Korea had begun to overtake important aspects of our study. In July we concluded that the political situation in Korea had changed so markedly that our findings would have to be updated. In early September, therefore, four of us returned to Korea for five days of discussions, again with a large number of people representing diverse views. The final meeting of our group took place in New York in late September 1987.

Our study could not have been carried out without the assistance of many individuals and organizations. Our greatest debt is to the many Koreans who generously and openly shared with us their insights and their hopes and fears. We thank also those Americans in Korea and in the United States who contributed to our study and the many people in Korea and the United States who assisted in arranging our activities.

The Korea study project has been most ably directed by Alan D. Romberg of the Council on Foreign Relations and Marshall M. Bouton of The Asia Society. We are deeply grateful to both for their excellent design and execution of every phase of the project, from the organization of our meetings to the drafting of this report. They were in every sense full participants in our effort.

Other members of the staffs of the Society and Council contributed valuably to the project. We thank particularly Lisa Molho and David Kellogg of the Council and Mari Maruyama and Linda Griffin Kean of the Asia Society. Susan Moffat of Columbia University was an especially effective rapporteur of our meetings and contributor to our drafting.

Funding for the Korea study project was provided by Patrick A. Gerschel, the Ford Foundation, the John D. and Catherine T. MacArthur Foundation, the Rockefeller Brothers Fund, and the Rockefeller Foundation. On behalf of the two sponsoring organizations as well as our group, I wish to express gratitude for this timely and generous support.

Finally, as chairman of the Korea study group, I should like to thank my fellow group members Robert B. Oxnam and Peter Tarnoff, presidents of The Asia Society and Council on Foreign Relations respectively, for their personal foresight in proposing this study and their organizations' initiative in sponsoring it. The experience has demonstrated the merits of the project and of the collaborative energy behind it.

All members of our group served purely in their individual capacities and not as representatives of their organizations. This report reflects the views of the group as a whole. No member, of course, endorses every statement or conclusion. But the thrust of the analysis is one in which we all share.

Kenneth W. Dam
Chairman
Korea Study Group

October 13, 1987

Members of the Korea Study Group

Members

Kenneth W. Dam (Chairman), *Vice President, Law & External Relations, IBM Corporation; Former Deputy Secretary of State*

William H. Gleysteen, Jr., *Director of Studies, Council on Foreign Relations; Former Ambassador to Korea*

Maurice R. Greenberg, *President & CEO, American International Group*

Henry Grunwald, *Editor-in-Chief, Time, Inc.*

Richard C. Holbrooke, *Managing Director, Shearson Lehman Brothers Inc.; Former Assistant Secretary of State for East Asian and Pacific Affairs*

Karen Elliott House, *Foreign Editor*, The Wall Street Journal (Ms. House participated in the study project but as a journalist refrains from associating with the conclusions of any group)

John Hughes, *Syndicated Columnist; Former Assistant Secretary of State for Public Affairs and State Department Spokesman*

Paul H. Kreisberg, *Senior Associate, Carnegie Endowment for International Peace; Former Director of Studies, Council on Foreign Relations*

William J. McDonough, *Vice Chairman, First Chicago Corporation*

Edward C. Meyer, *International Consultant; Former Chief of Staff, U.S. Army*

Robert B. Oxnam, *President, The Asia Society*

Dwight H. Perkins, *Director, Harvard Institute for International Development*

Robert A. Scalapino, *Robson Research Professor of Government, and Director, Institute of East Asian Studies, University of California*

KOREA
AT THE
CROSSROADS
Implications for American Policy

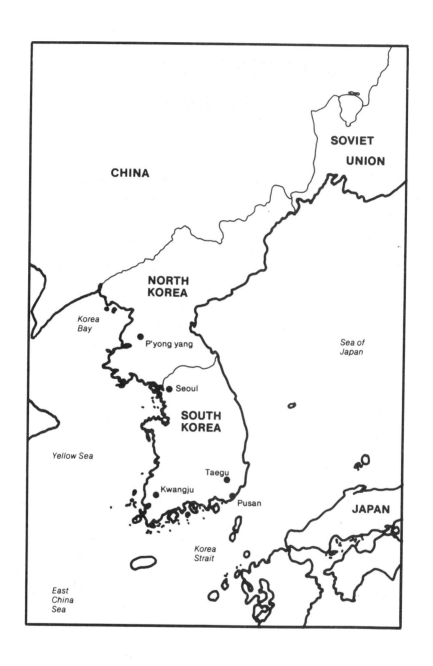

CHINA

SOVIET
UNION

NORTH
KOREA

Korea
Bay

P'yong yang

Sea of
Japan

Seoul

SOUTH
KOREA

Yellow Sea

Taegu

Kwangju

Pusan

JAPAN

Korea
Strait

East
China
Sea

Summary and Key Judgments

The Republic of Korea (ROK) stands at a historic turning point. Over the last 40 years it has traveled a difficult path from economic devastation to extraordinary accomplishment, from repressive rule to democratic opportunity. As they prepare to host the 1988 Seoul Olympics, the Korean people are justly proud of their achievements and are anxious for the international recognition those achievements merit.

In the next year or two, Korea faces a very delicate but crucial passage to a more representative system. For many years there has been growing resentment over military domination of politics. As the economy has grown, as the security situation has improved, and as education levels have risen, the Korean people's determination to choose their leaders through democratic elections has become a powerful force for change.

The presidential election in December 1987, along with the parliamentary elections in April 1988, are only the first steps in a very difficult but critical process of sharing power—not only between parties, but, with the substantial shift of prerogatives from the administration to the National Assembly, between branches of government as well.

If successful, not only will Koreans have broken with past precedent—the last two presidents were brought into office by military coups—they will have chosen a government they accept as legitimate and that hopefully will be responsive to their wishes.

Although power sharing may well result in less orderliness and efficiency throughout the society, it holds great promise for Korea's continuing economic strength and national security as well as for its political development.

There will inevitably be moments of tension—and setbacks—in the political transition, and success is far from assured. The prospects are significantly affected by historical experience. A tradition of authoritarian politics has its roots in over a thousand years of kingship and imperial rule, influenced heavily by the hierarchical values and obligations of Confucianism. In more modern times, and in the wake of colonial occupation and war in the first half of this century, this authoritarianism has been manifest through bureaucratic and military elites who have governed South Korea for the past 40 years.

A powerful nationalism has been forged through rugged opposition to historical pressures from Japan and China and, more recently, the Soviet Union and the Democratic People's Republic of Korea (DPRK). In the future, this sense of national identity may facilitate a degree of reconciliation with North Korea. Until now, however, its chief effect has been to serve as a potent source of unity in the South which sometimes bridges, or even disguises, deeper political rifts.

As a consequence, the ROK lacks a tradition of democracy, and it has not developed the political institutions and the habits of compromise and mutual trust that are needed to move politics beyond personalized contests for exclusive power. The landmark agreement between the ruling and opposition parties on constitutional change has inspired much hope, even euphoria. Nonetheless, a surprising number of Koreans remain nervous that, no matter who is elected, the situation may unravel, conceivably before the December 1987 presidential elections but more likely after the Olympics. They fear that dissidents, students, and labor groups could clash with military forces, or that a coup could emerge from disorder.

Koreans are gratified that the demonstrations in June resulted in an accord on direct presidential elections. Yet the middle class, whose backing was crucial to the success of those protests, remains essentially conservative and protective of its growing stake in economic stability. Thus there was great concern over the labor disorder last summer and the prospect that it might be exploited by radical students and dissident extremists. Some moderates even spoke tolerantly of the "cleansing effect" a brief military intervention could bring if things deteriorated further. Most, however, feared that such a confrontation would polarize Korean society, undercut economic growth, and damage ROK security.

The economy is strong, yet even without major political disruption it faces significant challenges in the years ahead. With the international environment becoming less friendly for exports, there are new pressures on Seoul to seek more balanced growth with less dependence on foreign markets. Moreover, although Korea has not suffered from the flagrant inequalities of wealth and the widespread gross corruption that have plagued other developing societies, there has been a growing perception of inequity in recent years. As unions and other interest groups gain more freedom, their efforts to address this sense of unfairness may lessen Korean economic competitiveness by reducing labor discipline, driving wage increases beyond productivity gains, diverting resources to less productive and more costly social welfare expenditures, and impinging on the government's ability to implement policy. Despite these potentially significant complications, by allowing people to identify with—rather than against—the government, we believe successful democratization would solidify the economic gains already achieved and would lay a sound basis for further development.

Confrontation with North Korea remains a serious concern. DPRK intrigues and subversive activities are always a potential danger, never more so than at this time of approaching political succession in the North. Nonetheless, joint ROK–U.S. deterrence against a major attack continues to hold, and North Korea's allies in the Soviet Union and China have manifest a clear interest in discouraging an outbreak of hostilities.

The stakes for the United States are high. The 42 million South Korean people live on a strategically located peninsula, and America has been deeply involved since the end of World War II in defending and preserving their independence and promoting their prosperity, from which both countries have benefited substantially. That involvement has been reinforced by the large number of Koreans educated in the United States and the one million who live and work here.

Success in opening the Korean political process and in adjusting the economy to the new realities will lead to an improvement in the human rights situation, including labor rights, and may help temper the still limited but growing mood of anti-Americanism which feeds on nationalistic resentment of continuing dependence on the United States. Korean democratization will also reaffirm the belief of Americans that the human and material sacrifices made on Korea's behalf over the past 40 years have been worthwhile, and that the continuing U.S. treaty commitment to ROK security—with 157,000 American casualties in the Korean War and 40,000 American troops still there—serves not only Korean but also American interests. Failure—particularly extreme violence on the streets or a military coup—would have the opposite effect, chilling U.S.–Korean relations and presenting the United States with difficult and unpleasant choices.

Even under current circumstances, it has been suggested by a few Americans that the United States consider withdrawing its forces unless Korea makes substantial political progress. Despite our strong support for democratization, we believe such an effort to use the U.S. defense commitment as leverage on domestic issues would be seriously misplaced. It would tempt North Korean meddling and enhance the chances of a military crackdown in the South. Except among some students in Korea, we found strong support for the bilateral security relationship and concern over any suggestion it might be weakened.

On the other hand, certain aspects of that relationship do merit adjustment or at least reconsideration even now, not to exert pressure, but rather to take account of growing Korean national pride and real military strength. We believe the overall commander of both the U.N. Command and the U.S.–ROK Combined Forces Command should remain an American. It would nevertheless be appropriate after 1988 to place ground forces, both American and Korean, under the operational control of a Korean in peacetime. Giving greater responsibility to Koreans would both reflect and encourage their increased professionalism, distancing the military further from politics. And it could reduce misperceptions that the United States has control over the use of ROK forces for domestic purposes.

Looking to the longer run, the United States and South Korea may want to consider reconfiguring U.S. forces so as to better complement ROK strengths, placing greater emphasis on American air and naval power and on Korean ground forces. Any such change would need to be carried out in full, mutual consultation and in a manner that would both underscore the unambiguous U.S. commitment and maintain effective deterrence on the peninsula.

The United States and South Korea have a common interest in easing tensions and improving relations with North Korea. We applaud both Seoul's generally sensible, confidence-building approach to North-South dialogue and the U.S. support for it. The ROK's confident handling of that relationship reflects its real accomplishments and its growing underlying strength as compared with the DPRK. We encourage Washington and Seoul to demonstrate creativity and flexibility in their continuing search for ways to reduce confrontation with North Korea and to revitalize the dialogue after South Korean domestic politics have settled down. We recognize, however, that responsibility for tensions on the peninsula lies primarily with the North and that, without a change in Pyongyang's attitude, little progress can be expected.

From now on, the United States will find it even more difficult to cope with the problem of Korean sensibilities and the need for occasional pressure in the economic relationship. In the very short term, in order to avoid getting caught up in the heated political climate, the United States should refrain, until after the presidential elections, from pressing new economic demands, specifically new Section 301 cases under the Trade Act of 1974 for relief from unfair trade practices. For quite different—economic—reasons, it might also be appropriate to assess the longer-run effects of the new Korean economic climate on ROK competitiveness before pressing for further rapid currency appreciation.

Having said that, failure to face up to trade and investment problems, including the need for Seoul to meaningfully open its markets, will seriously damage the U.S. administration's efforts to resist protectionist legislation, including measures aimed directly at Korea. We are particularly concerned that, devoted as senior Korean policymakers and technocrats may be to economic liberalization, some American companies still encounter legal, regulatory, bureaucratic, and other barriers to actual transactions. These issues may become more difficult to resolve in a more democratic Korean environment in which interest groups, including labor unions and members of the National Assembly, will likely become more vocal and more influential. Nonetheless, in light of Korea's growing trade surplus with the United States, and at a time of record U.S. global trade deficits, resolution of these problems will be important to effective management of the ever more complex economic relationship between the two countries.

In sum, Korean developments across the board are impressive, but much remains to be done to stay on track. Bilateral relations will need to be adjusted to take account of the new political and economic situation in both countries. South Korea is not so fragile that it will shatter at the least whisper of U.S. criticism or pressure. And fortunately, the current political contest is essentially a struggle for power rather than a contention between different visions for Korea that could dramatically affect U.S. interests. Still, Korea is at a moment of transition, and its success or failure is of great consequence to the United States. To facilitate a successful passage, the United States needs to pursue careful and well-coordinated policies that are reasonable and clearly defined and that are implemented with consistency and due sensitivity to Korean realities.

Americans should have no illusion about the real limits on their influence, but they should not overlook the opportunities that do exist to play a positive role. Particularly over the past several months, while remaining neutral among candidates, the United States has strongly backed democratization in Korea. Washington has unequivocally opposed a repetition of the past pattern of military intervention in politics. We strongly endorse these positions and believe they have helped in some measure.

Setbacks in Korea's democratic course are inevitable. Some may put American resolve to a severe test. It will be essential that the United States remain solidly behind its current policy. Koreans of all political persuasions should understand the United States will support their efforts at democratization, even through the difficult times. But they should also know that reversion to previous cycles of provocation and forcible response, of blind hostility descending into violent confrontation, will bring consequences for U.S.–Korean relations that will likely be much greater than at previous times of strain.

If all goes well in Korea, American public attention may recede after the 1988 Seoul Olympics. That would be unfortunate because the importance of the United States and Korea to one another will, if anything, grow rather than diminish. Today, Korea's political weakness has the potential to jeopardize its economy and its security position, and it strains the overall U.S.–Korean relationship. By the same token, despite the greater degree of indiscipline that democratization will bring, the resulting political strengthening—with a new emphasis on coalitions and compromise—should also strengthen and help open up Korea's economy and reinforce its security, thereby benefiting the overall relationship. The lesser degree of orderliness among competing Korean interests will doubtless generate new domestic problems, and increasing nationalism on both sides may create new, and sometimes serious, tensions between the two countries. If handled intelligently by both, however, these developments should provide the foundation for a truly productive partnership in the years ahead.

1
Politics

*C*onflicting pulls between almost equally powerful forces for change and conservation explain much of the tension and abrupt development that has marked Korean politics this year. Korea's astonishing economic success has given most people, especially a rapidly growing "middle class," a substantial stake in the system. During the past 25 years, the 60 to 70 percent of Koreans who now put themselves in that category, as well as the large block of farmers and unskilled workers, have been generally wary of student activists and other agitators. Despite manifest resentment, they have tolerated a substantial degree of political repression and even brutality by the government. Moreover, the clear and present danger from North Korea, a scant 30 miles from the capital city of Seoul, where one-fourth of the population resides and where much economic activity is centered, has reinforced this preserving instinct, especially among those who lived through the trauma and devastation of the 1950–53 Korean War.

At the same time, democracy in one form or another has been a goal of many Koreans since the Republic's founding. The same economic miracle that raised per capita GNP from under $100 in 1960 to over $2,300 in 1986, has contributed to Koreans' frustration with the regime's repressive policies and demands for political liberalization. As basic needs have been satisfied, as educational levels have risen (Korea now has 98 percent literacy and one million college students), and as nationalistic pride has grown, the Korean people have increasingly come to believe in their ability to govern themselves.

Pressure for democratic development is often focused on the question of legitimacy. With only brief exceptions, Korea has not experienced an open political process. Successive governments have come into power by military coup and have ruled through an authoritarian structure in which the military has wielded an ultimate veto. Although many Koreans acknowledge the economic and social progress achieved, the administration of President Chun Doo Hwan has never been accepted as "legitimate" because of the way it came to power and because of its behavior since. For the most part, Koreans are only minimally impressed that, having seized power by force following the assassination of Park Chung Hee in 1979, Chun will leave office voluntarily in February 1988 after a single seven-year term. Most people feel their country has reached a stage where it should have a government elected by a democratic process without military interference.

Despite the clarity of this popular message about democracy and legitimacy, actual behavior in Korea has been heavily influenced by limited choice, external constraints, and considerable fickleness in attitudes. Pressures for change sometimes spread rapidly and unpredictably, as they did this past summer. The objective then was democratization. But if events threaten to run out of control, attitudes of many people may shift back in conservative directions, and the confusing pattern may lead both the government and opposition elements into dangerous miscalculations about public support.

The demographic shift in South Korea has contributed to growing tension between those focusing on stability and those looking toward democratization. More than 60 percent of the population is now under 30 years of age, over 40 percent in the politically active 15- to 29-year-old age group alone. Not only are these often idealistic younger people well educated, but they did not experience, or do not recall, the hardships of the war and its aftermath, and they do not take as seriously as their elders the danger from the North. Indeed, as the ROK's economy has strengthened, and along with it South Korean military power, the government's continued citation of the North Korean threat has lost much of its credibility as a justification for the denial of political liberties. This is true despite repeated assassinations and infiltration and a continuing military build-up by Pyongyang.

There are other important characteristics of Korean politics. Virtually since the establishment of the Republic of Korea in 1948, political activity has centered around factionalized parties bound by personal loyalties rather than by ideologies or programs. Despite the sometimes sharp differences in rhetoric between political leaders, who cast disputes in terms of principle—of black and white, with little gray—the struggle has not been so much a clash of radically different visions for Korea as a contention for power. Moreover, politics have operated in a highly centralized structure dominated by the leader of the national government, leaving the opposition with no experience in governance and intensifying a Korean resistance to political compromise. As a consequence, both the traditions of give and take and the development of modern political institutions have been stymied.

Increasingly, Korean academics, journalists, and even younger politicians have come to identify an unwillingness to compromise and a lack of sincerity, credibility, and mutual trust among political activists as important stumbling blocks to political development. The degree of fear and distrust between opposing camps is profound. Opposition and dissident forces are convinced that only massive displays of popular opposition have—or will—force the government to change and that nothing can be left to trust. The government and its supporters view oppositionists for the most part as either weak and incompetent or dangerous to the security of the state.

Although Korea does not suffer from the ethnic and religious animosities that divide many other societies, there is a significant element of regional antagonism that exacerbates political tensions. Movement toward autonomous local government was cut off after 1960. Thus, pending developments promised on this front in 1988, people who have felt underrepresented at the national level have had no effective vehicle except confrontation to focus attention on their complaints.

Student activism has been a prominent factor in Korean politics for over 400 years, and in modern times it played a central role in bringing down the authoritarian and corrupt regime of Syngman Rhee in 1960. Students are in the forefront of today's protest movement as well. Most are idealistic and politically inexperienced, and only 1 to 2 percent are true radicals working for revolution. Still, that relatively small group is hard-core and well organized, and concern for stability, not only among the military but also among other segments of the population, often provides conservative leaders with considerable justification for hard-line policies.

This situation has been complicated by the role of religious leaders, especially in the Christian community. The bulk of Protestant ministers have taken conservative stands, reflecting the outlook of their parishioners. Some however, have been deeply involved in anti-government protest, garnering particular support in this June's campaign for direct elections. Their image was tarnished, however, by the perception that they had played an agitator's role during labor unrest later in the summer. A number of priests have also played an activist role. But Catholic leaders, especially Cardinal Kim Sou Hwan, have taken a liberalizing but less openly confrontational approach and have had an impact disproportionate to their small ministry (5 percent of the population).

The Japanese occupation (1910–45) and the rule of repressive authoritarian governments since that time have effectively cut off incremental liberalization and political evolution that might have fostered the institutions and patterns of democratic government to supplant authoritarian traditions and values developed during a thousand years of imperial rule and Confucianism. Even the development of political thought has been caught in a time warp. Naïve idealism and such propositions as "dependency theory," which have long since given way to more realistic and pragmatic approaches in a number of other countries, are just now working their way through dissident intellectual circles in Korea. As we discuss at the end of this section, this is in part an outgrowth of increasing nationalism and has contributed to the rise of anti-Americanism in some quarters.

Having identified some of the key forces in Korean politics that will have effect well beyond the next election, we turn to a discussion of the crossroads Korea now faces and how it has gotten to this critical juncture.

February 1985–April 1986: Setting the Scene

A new chapter in Korean politics was opened by the National Assembly elections of February 1985 in which previously banned politicians were allowed to participate. Although divisions among the opposition gave Chun's Democratic Justice Party (DJP) a plurality, opposition candidates from various parties won the majority of election contests, primarily in the cities. Even with the prescribed allocation of a major block of seats to the leading party (an obvious constitutional device to compensate for the electorate's traditionally lukewarm support for the government), the DJP lacked a two-thirds majority. This meant that the government could not, for example, amend the constitution at will.

Sensing its new strength, the opposition immediately began to press forcefully for a direct presidential election, attempting to eliminate the indirect electoral college system. The existing system, with over 5,000 electors who were not legally bound to vote for the candidate they claimed to support, was generally discredited throughout the body politic as inherently manipulable by the government and biased in favor of the ruling party. Although many members of the Korean opposition had long favored a parliamentary cabinet system over any kind of presidential system, they reversed their position to capture the apparent public mood for direct choice of the nation's leader. Moreover, long-time opposition leader Kim Dae Jung had returned to Korea just four days before the elections after two years of "medical treatment" in the United States. Kim had won about 45 percent of the vote against Park Chung Hee in the 1971 presidential election, and he saw his strength in an appeal to "the people," rather than through insider politics where rival opposition leader Kim Young Sam excelled.

President Chun at first refused to countenance any amendment to the existing system, hoping to guarantee the safe transfer of power to a chosen successor and wanting to avoid political disruption prior to the September 1988 Olympics. Chun's scenario was not to be, however, and—possibly influenced by the ouster of Philippine President Ferdinand Marcos in February 1986—he announced on April 30, 1986, that he would accept any new system on which the parties could agree. The government, perhaps feeling its fate was best assured through its political control in local election districts (especially in over-represented rural ones), abandoned its traditional support of a presidential system in favor of a parliamentary cabinet government.

With these opposite positions, and with neither side controlling enough votes to push its version through, the scene was set for confrontation and stalemate.

April 1986–June 1987: Stalemate and Confrontation

In the absence of a tradition of compromise (even many Koreans who profess to believe in accommodation admit they think of a compromiser as a "traitor"), it was not surprising that there was no progress toward a mutually acceptable solution over the next twelve months. But there was frustration and even anger. When we began our study in early 1987, blame seemed rather evenly directed by the Korean people toward the government and the opposition: at the government for not implementing a program of democratization that would have been valuable in and of itself and would have given the opposition a face-saving opportunity to acquiesce in a parliamentary system; at the opposition for not facing the fact that they lacked the power to win in the National Assembly and thus should settle for a reasonable deal. An effort at compromise in late 1986 by one opposition leader was stymied by the two Kims, who subsequently founded their own new party in April 1987 based on unwavering advocacy of a system of direct presidential election.

This series of events set the scene for a dazzling display of political fireworks in mid-1987 which culminated in the stunning reversal by the DJP in June that opened the door to the election scheduled to take place this December.

In brief, Chun sought to play on public frustration over opposition intransigence and to capitalize on opposition disarray by declaring on April 13 that it was "too late" to continue consideration of constitutional change and that further debate would not only be fruitless but harmful. Therefore, he said, he was suspending dialogue on any amendment until after the peaceful transfer of power in February 1988 and the Seoul Olympics.

His action backfired. With as much as eight months remaining before an election had to take place, Chun's rationale of time constraints was unpersuasive, even to DJP members. The decision was seen by the president's critics as "proof" that he had never intended to allow change. It also came just as middle-class outrage was aroused by the revelation of a police coverup of true responsibility for the torture-murder of a college student four months earlier. And when demonstrations were organized by the opposition parties, students, and other dissident elements to protest the June 10 nomination of DJP Chairman Roh Tae Woo as his party's presidential candidate, the excessive use of tear gas by police angered that same middle class even further, causing them to lend support to the demonstrators.

Despite a rear-guard action by Chun to stem the tide of protest, it became clear that Roh's legitimacy as president would be challenged by the fact that he would have been the sole candidate in an indirect election that had been discredited beforehand and that had been boycotted by the opposition. Moreover, the prospect of continuing demonstrations over a period of months, and of tear gas clouds lying heavily across the city, threatened eventual cancellation of the Seoul Olympics. More than simply a political failure, this would have been a national disgrace.

On June 29, Roh surprised almost everybody by announcing he would recommend that Chun accept a direct presidential election, that he offer amnesty and restoration of full rights to political prisoners and others including Kim Dae Jung (who had been barred from formal political activity since his return because of his 1980 conviction on sedition charges), and that he adopt a series of other "democratization" measures. Roh said that if Chun refused he would withdraw as a candidate and resign all other public positions. The president announced his acceptance on July 1.

Although denied by Chun, it is widely believed that around June 18 the president seriously considered imposing a state of emergency just short of martial law, a so-called garrison state. Some Koreans also say, however, that he did not do so because the military made clear their refusal to become involved in an essentially political confrontation and that this contributed centrally to the subsequent efforts at political compromise leading up to June 29.

Fall 1987: Sober Attitudes

The dramatic turn of events this summer has transformed the nature of the debate in Korea. Though we detected no increase in respect for politicians or politics, anger and despair have been replaced with organizing activities by the parties and efforts by the candidates to bone up on the issues.

Nonetheless, by the time some of us returned to Seoul in early September, the opposition's euphoria, which had erupted in the wake of "victory" on the issue of direct presidential election, and the elation in Roh's camp over his brilliant stroke on June 29, had given way to a degree of anxiety. Across the political spectrum, many worried whether the election results would be honored by the losing side or whether another cycle of military intervention might not be brewing.

Contributing to this unease was the fact that the heady spirit of "democracy" after June 29 had opened the door to over 3,000 strikes by laborers previously prohibited from such actions. Most Koreans with whom we spoke—even technocrats who had worked to restrain wage increases and businessmen who had thereby profited—accepted the existence of valid workers' grievances. But many felt the specific demands were unrealistic, and they were concerned by the absence of guidelines and mechanisms to facilitate negotiations. Whereas the government had been blamed for obstructing democracy—including workers' rights—a scant three months before, it was now accused by many people of failing to intervene to help calm the situation, at least by establishing "rules of the game."

There were two areas of particular concern to many people. They worried about the economic effects on Korea's competitiveness and, hence, their own prosperity. But more fundamentally, they feared the violence and arrests and charges of existing or potential student and other dissident agitation would lead to renewed rioting and an eventual military crackdown.

Some Koreans confirmed our impression that the middle class's tolerance of violence is now higher than before the June demonstrations. There is also a higher threshold on the government side, as indicated by Roh Tae Woo and the minister of defense, who both stated firmly that the military would not act without support of the people. Disturbingly, however, a number of business leaders, conservative politicians, and others spoke in terms that seemed to invite military intervention. They charged that rabble-rousers outside the labor movement were stirring up workers, not for the sake of bread and butter issues with which the workers themselves were concerned, but to press a political agenda of social upheaval. And military leaders who expressed firm opposition to arbitrary army involvement in politics spoke in the next breath of their responsibility to maintain public order and protect property, citing American precedents. Even some moderate opponents of the government implied that a quick military "police" operation (as opposed to another coup) might not be all that bad.

In turn, opposition politicians and dissidents assured us that they were not agitating the workers and that the radical students— who, they acknowledged, represented a genuine threat to stability if labor unrest continued—had not yet had a significant impact. But, some charged, the government was promoting activities by radicals in order to create a pretext for military intervention. This suspicion receded in the early fall with settlement of most strikes, but it remains a potential concern for the next round of wage negotiations when the radicals may be better organized.

In early September, agreement was reached between the political parties on the terms of the constitutional amendment for a direct presidential election. This included settlement of such controversial issues as the term of office (a single five-year term), labor rights and freedom of the press (to be guaranteed), and the handling of reference to the Kwangju incident of May 1980, in which over 200 Koreans were killed in clashes between demonstrators and armed forces (no specific reference was to be made). But even this compromise did not totally reassure people about the volatile mix of labor turmoil, student activism, and military restiveness.

The concern was further heightened as Kim Dae Jung withheld his decision on running for the presidency until the last minute. People doubted the military would tolerate his candidacy and believed the army would surely prevent his taking office, convinced he was soft on communism, likely to weaken national security, and certain to seek vengeance for past maltreatment. Despite later denials and clarifications by Roh Tae Woo and Defense Minister Chung Ho Yong, it is widely believed that the army chief of staff, in a conversation with reporters, made a statement containing a veiled threat against a Kim Dae Jung candidacy.

While emphasizing that he will not yield to military intimidation, Kim says that the military and their conservative civilian colleagues have misunderstood or purposely misconstrued his stands against authoritarian rule and for reconciliation with the North. He professes with some vehemence that he is stoutly anti-communist, a strong supporter of the military in their national security role though totally opposed to any role in politics, and a firm backer of the U.S.–ROK alliance. He also claims he will not seek punishment of those responsible for his kidnapping, arrest, and torture or even for the deaths in Kwangju.

The fundamental characteristics of Korean political life remain problematic, including mistrust, a lack of credibility, regional loyalties, and the weakness of institutions which leaves them unable to carry differences beyond the realm of personalized confrontation. Idealistic young people, dissatisfied with the inequities in society, frustrated at the slow pace of political liberalization, and enlivened by a new sense of nationalism, aspire to the model of a previous generation in forcing dramatic change. And while there is no convincing evidence of institutional links between North Korea and the core group of dedicated radicals who seek to take advantage of these feelings, they hold similar revolutionary objectives.

On the other side, most in the military cherish their professionalism, resent the tarnishing effect of the Kwangju incident on their reputation, and support civilian, democratic government. But mistrust of the opposition and fear that social chaos would tempt North Korean intervention still animate some in key positions. And, as noted, even some middle-of-the-road figures who are strongly opposed to military domination of the political scene did not recoil at the prospect of some "policing" action by the military if conditions continued to deteriorate.

A number of Koreans state quite openly that even if the election goes forward—no matter who is elected—some combination of these elements, compounded by the continuing instinct against compromise, will lead to an "unraveling" not long after the Olympics. Others are more sanguine and point out that since the government began to play a more active mediating role in labor disputes in late August, problems in that area have become manageable and will neither afford radicals an opening they can exploit nor provoke military intervention. They point hopefully to Korea's underlying economic and military strength and the growing political maturity manifest in events since June.

The December 1987 Election

It is not possible for foreigners—and perhaps not even for Koreans—to predict with confidence what will finally determine how the voters will make their decision. The impulse against military rule and feelings of vengeance will compete with a fear of disorder and of the unknown. The rules established for the campaign, and even the list of candidates, will not be fixed until the last minute. Ultimately, the election may turn on the sense voters have of who is better able to move the political process forward.

At this point, one can identify a number of factors that will come into play. First is the question of the fairness of the electoral process. The DJP is not going to relinquish the advantages of incumbency, such as the ability to use government programs to benefit specific constituencies. But they have pledged free and fair elections. DJP leaders say that they understand the need to meet the challenge of legitimacy, and thus, some told us, they would accept virtually any opposition proposal regarding balloting and the counting of votes. Opposition reactions range from mild skepticism to disbelief. In any case, members of the opposition say, the unfairness will come in more subtle ways, and some seem determined to charge fraud, whatever the facts, if Roh wins.

The issue of press freedom, once prominent, seems to have faded. Opposition figures told us in the spring that the government control over television posed the greatest problem. Ironically, the DJP is now strongly advocating the opposition's use of TV, and particularly televised debates, because they have concluded that Roh Tae Woo's cool demeanor is much more suited to the medium than is Kim Dae Jung's ardent rhetoric or Kim Young Sam's hesitant style.

Regionalism will play a major role, but exactly how is hard to tell. On the one hand, candidates from rival areas could be pitted against one another, turning the election into a regional contest. On the other, if there is no candidate from the long-neglected southwestern Cholla area—Kim Dae Jung's home base and site of the Kwangju incident—the people in that region will feel deprived of the opportunity to exercise a fair share of power. In any case, it was manifestly clear in the analysis of election possibilities presented to us by all sides that regional loyalty is central to each candidate's campaign strategy.

As noted earlier, reaction to the military role in politics will be an important aspect of the voters' decision. To deal with the opposition charge that he represents a continuation of the illegitimate tradition of military rule, Roh Tae Woo will have the delicate task of distancing himself from Chun Doo Hwan while not totally alienating him. Roh will no doubt argue that, not only did he have the vision to cut the Gordian knot and open the way to democratization, but as a former general he is far better placed to understand—and reassure—the military, and to stem any inclination on their part to intervene. Nonetheless, hard-line measures continuing to emanate from the presidential Blue House, including the arrest of relatively moderate student leaders, reveal the existence of powerful forces that are uncomfortable with the post–June 29 evolution and that wish to rein in Roh. This only reinforces the reluctance of many Koreans to trust the fairness of the system and heightens their concern about a military role. This will compound Roh's "legitimacy" problem, especially if he is elected by less than a majority due to multiple candidates.

Specific political or economic issues seem unlikely to figure importantly in the vote, although each side will, of course, have a platform with different stands on such questions as social welfare, reunification, and U.S.–ROK command relationships. The opposition will presumably stake out a populist position, including a more cautious attitude toward economic liberalization and market opening. The DJP will brand the opposition as inexperienced and unqualified to govern and will accuse it of espousing vaguely dangerous economic and security policies. The opposition will likely respond that of course they have no experience in governing—they've been shut out of power by dictatorship for 40 years! But, they will probably argue, they were the ones who backed the people's demand for a direct presidential election and had the courage to see it through to success.

We were struck by the concerns of moderate Koreans who worry that radical opinion is not given representation within the current political system and, thus shut out, can have no expression but in the street. At the same time, the opposition's desire to exploit dissident or even radical forces without becoming their captive will be one of their most difficult dilemmas. They have frequently enlisted the activists against the government. However, as we have already noted, many of those activists do not share the more modest—and moderate—objectives of the politicians. Once loosed, they have sometimes proved impossible to control short of the sort of forceful government intervention which, at this stage, could destroy the fragile balance that is allowing democratization to go forward.

The U.S. Role in Korean Politics

The United States was central to the recovery of Korean independence after World War II, the maintenance of that independence in the Korean War, and economic development ever since—first largely through aid, more recently through trade. (All economic and grant or concessional military assistance was phased out long ago, although guaranteed credits for military purchases at commercial rates continued until last year.) Given the North-South confrontation and the continuing concentration of DPRK forces just north of the Demilitarized Zone (DMZ), some 40,000 U.S. forces are still stationed in Korea (down from 64,000 in the late 1960s).

This role has given the United States a special place in the ROK and in the minds of the Korean people. With the passage of time, however, memories have faded and constraints have eased. Despite genuine feelings of appreciation and friendship, Korea's continuing dependence on the United States, in the face of growing ROK capabilities, has stirred nationalistic resentment.

This ambivalence will continue and probably grow, giving rise to further anti-Americanism. It is compounded by the growing view, particularly among oppositionists and younger people, that the

United States is selfishly pursuing its own interests without much concern for theirs. They feel that the United States has not lived up to its responsibilities by identifying itself with a series of illegitimate and repressive governments since 1948.

Especially since Washington started to apply pressure on trade and other economic issues two years ago, Americans are seen as self-centered and irresponsible. Arguing that the United States has already shown itself to be an unfaithful ally (in Vietnam), students told us America should reduce its military presence as soon as possible, while backing off from unfair economic demands and staying out of Korean politics.

An increasing number of younger Koreans have blamed the United States for "creating a divided Korea" and for "perpetuating" it. Even some officials, who know better, have echoed this charge, probably as a way of venting frustration over recent pressures from Washington on trade and especially democratization issues. Although anti-Americanism is not widespread, it has a certain resonance that student activists are currently exploiting and that even responsible leaders occasionally cannot refrain from tapping.

Moderates reject this negative view and welcome U.S. support for political liberalization. But they throw up their hands in despair at what they see as the conflicting American demand for economic liberalization. Pluralism will inevitably lead to greater Korean protectionism in their view; the United States should understand this, they say, and ease economic pressure.

Whether welcomed or scorned, American influence is clearly perceived by Koreans as a crucial factor in their domestic politics. We address this issue again in the discussion of U.S. policy at the end of this report, but generally speaking, we found the degree of influence ascribed to the United States to be exaggerated. Nonetheless, it appears virtually impossible to convince Koreans of this, so the United States will have to deal with both the reality of its limited influence and the perception of a larger role.

2
The Economy and U.S.–Korea Economic Relations

*T*he Korean economy is one of the most successful in the world. Over the last quarter century, Korea's annual growth in real GNP has averaged over 8 percent. In the same period the share of manufacturing in the economy has doubled. Exports and imports have risen from about 24 percent of GNP to about 82 percent, making Korea the world's twelfth largest trading nation. In 1986 Korea passed yet another economic milestone as it recorded its first merchandise trade surplus—$3.5 billion—and its first significant current account surplus—$4.6 billion.

The impact of this economic transformation on Korean society has been profound. Korea has changed from a rural society into a largely urban society, with a quarter of its 42 million people now living in Seoul. The distribution of the fruits of Korean economic growth has been widespread, especially as compared with that of other developing countries, although there are persistent differences in wealth and income. Unemployment has fallen from 7.7 percent in 1964 to 3.8 percent in 1986. Korean enrollment in higher education (now at 28 percent) has produced a large pool of professional and technical manpower. As a result of these changes, Korea's middle class has grown rapidly, and the society once known as the "hermit kingdom" has become increasingly international. Over the last several years, for example, Seoul has been the venue for a number of major international meetings.

The causes of Korea's "economic miracle" are numerous and complex. Most significantly, government policies have been generally effective in promoting growth through exports and foreign borrowing, and the global economic environment, in particular the open international trading system, has favored rapid export growth. Economic success and political stability in Korea have reinforced each other through much of the last 25 years, allowing the government to take bold moves with respect to the economy and to implement even unpopular policies. But it is important to realize that despite the overall record, Korean policies have sometimes failed, and the economy has not always performed well. The economy now must adapt to new and more complex domestic and international conditions, including labor unrest and growing wage demands at home and increased competition, rising protectionism, and greater demands for market-opening measures abroad.

The Korean government began to emphasize export development in the 1960s, providing powerful incentives for labor-intensive manufactured exports. This policy reflected the country's lack of natural resources and its limited domestic market, took advantage of Korea's highly disciplined and relatively well-educated labor force, and depended upon access to the American market.

By the mid to late 1970s, however, faulty government policies began to impede economic progress. The government's decision to emphasize heavy industry produced a number of bad investments in such major industries as heavy machinery that still plague the economy. Misguided government intervention in economic decision-making also impaired the economy's ability to adjust to the external shocks of the oil crisis and world recession. These policies, along with the political uncertainty following President Park's assassination, bad weather, and falling demand for exports, contributed to a sharp economic setback in 1980, when Korea experienced a negative growth rate of 4.8 percent and an inflation rate of 28.7 percent.

Subsequently the adoption of more market-oriented policies and the good fortune of the "three lows"—the low dollar, low oil prices, and low interest rates—have helped Korea return to a path of rapid growth and price stability. Gross national product grew at 12.5 percent in 1986 and at over 15 percent in the first half of 1987, while consumer price increases remained below 3 percent in 1984, 1985, and

1986. Beginning in 1986 Korea began also to reduce its large foreign debt from the high of almost $47 billion in 1985 to about $39 billion by mid-1987.

Although Korea's extraordinary economic performance has made it a leader among the newly industrialized countries, it has not yet joined the ranks of the developed countries. Per capita income is one-sixth that of Japan, and while the standard of living of the middle class in Seoul has risen sharply, it clearly remains below that of Japan. Although Koreans often overemphasize the fragility of their economy, it *is* heavily dependent on trade with only two countries—the United States and Japan. Many key export-oriented industries rely on imports of capital and intermediate goods, are heavily indebted, and operate on thin margins. Korean industry is also heavily concentrated in a few huge conglomerates. The rapidity with which the labor unrest of summer 1987 affected export performance (perhaps only temporarily) suggests that the economy does in fact remain quite vulnerable to internal and external shocks.

The caveats surrounding Korea's economic prospects, however, do not justify the degree of Korean protectionism that exists today. Continued growth, which is essential to Korea's political stability and international security, will require even greater policy sophistication and flexibility in the years ahead.

Future Challenges and Responses

The Korean economy is now entering a critical new phase in its development. As policymakers and business leaders look to the 1990s they foresee multiple challenges to past economic policies and patterns. Korea's dependence on trade is threatened by rising protectionism in its key markets and by growing competition from less developed countries in major labor-intensive exports such as textiles, footwear, and light manufactures. Korea's foreign debt is not large relative to its ability to pay, but the reduction of that debt is now seen as politically important.

As the events of the summer of 1987 have made clear, labor-management relations now must be a high priority for policymakers and business leaders. At the same time, economic success has given rise to popular expectations for an improved quality of life and an expanded social welfare system. Finally, Korea's economic policy process is bound to become more complex as its economy becomes more diverse and its politics more open.

To meet these challenges, Korea's economic policymakers are seeking to develop a more balanced economy. Pursuing policies first adopted eight to ten years ago, they propose to reduce Korea's vulnerability in trade by encouraging the diversification of exports and imports and by expanding the domestic market. They also foresee structural adjustment in industry, emphasizing the development of small and medium-size enterprises and of knowledge-intensive industries. They plan to invest in infrastructure and social welfare programs and to give greater scope to private economic decision-making.

The key to this more balanced approach, according to Korean policymakers, is the gradual liberalization of the economy. Policy initiatives have been developed which, if fully implemented and complemented by corollary measures, promise considerable change. But it is also apparent that these policies do not go far enough, especially in opening Korea's market, and that the obstacles to further liberalization are many.

The most pressing task is the management of Korea's growing trade and current account surpluses, which threaten to disrupt economic relations with the United States. In April 1987 the Korean government unveiled a package of measures with the announced goal of containing the annual current account surplus at the 1986 level of $5 billion over the next several years. The government proposed to expand and diversify imports by accelerating the removal of import restrictions, by providing special foreign currency loans for imports, and by promoting imports from the United States rather than from Japan. It imposed quantitative restrictions on certain low value–added exports. And it sought to stimulate domestic demand by increasing public sector investments.

These measures, while welcome, are probably not sufficient. Before the labor difficulties of the summer exerted their depressant effect on the economy, Korea's current account surplus was headed toward an annual total of $8–10 billion, its trade surplus with the United States threatened to surpass that of 1986, and its trade deficit with Japan continued to grow.

The principal criticism of the new liberalizing policies is that they focus on *managing trade* rather than on opening the Korean market to foreign goods and services. Lifting import restrictions is not likely to have much impact, for instance, unless it is accompanied by changes in local laws and regulations that make it difficult for some foreign companies actually to operate and sell in Korea. For example, Korean government regulations make it difficult for foreign companies to store large inventories of consumer goods in Korea, thus increasing product costs and lengthening delivery times.

More broadly, these and other liberalizing policies are not easily implemented. While top technocrats clearly believe that liberalization is in Korea's interest, many lower-level bureaucrats, business leaders, and politicians oppose it. Saving foreign exchange and controlling economic decisions are habits ingrained in the bureaucracy. Business executives argue that they are not ready to compete with U.S. firms. They point to the generally positive role that they believe the Korean government has long played in the economy. Members of the National Assembly explained to us that Korea's farmers must continue to be protected. Opposition leaders, even those who in principle favor market opening, expressed concern about the impact of liberalization on the small and medium-size businesses which they believe have been neglected by the government. Special concern is also voiced about liberalization of the financial sector because, it is argued, Korean financial institutions are not well developed and have recently been shaken by several scandals. Finally, despite the confidence of government planners that they are on the right track, even many of them express the concern that too rapid liberalization would endanger the trade and current account surpluses that Korea has just begun to enjoy.

The surpluses, in this view, are critical to other major policy goals. First and foremost, public concern over the nation's large debt remains high, and the government wants to bring it down to a "safer level." Very few Koreans argue, however, that the debt presents a serious economic problem at present levels. Second, funds are needed to invest in the continued modernization of industry. Korea is losing its comparative advantage in certain major industries, such as textiles and shoes, and must move into higher value–added industries if it is to remain internationally competitive. But it is important to recognize, as some Koreans do, that the future competitiveness of Korean firms and products will depend heavily on an opening of Korea's markets.

The widespread resistance to liberalization springs in part from a sense of economic vulnerability and a desire to control and protect Korea's economic interests. Such a view is perhaps understandable in light of how recently the economy emerged from its less developed state, but it conflicts with the requirement for policies that are more appropriate and beneficial to Korea's new, more advanced economic status.

Another challenge for the Korean economy in the years ahead is to bring about a distribution of economic power and income that will be politically acceptable. As we have noted above, the benefits of economic success have been relatively widely shared. But in recent years public concern over the concentration of economic power in a few hands has increased. Much of this concern focuses on the *chaebol*, or large industrial conglomerates, which accounted for 40.7 percent of sales and 18.6 percent of employment in 1982 and are seen by many Koreans as having acquired their position through government favoritism and foreign borrowing.

Some Koreans argue further that the dominance of the conglomerates hinders Korea's ability to adapt to rapid change in the international economy. As noted above, the government has begun to address the problem through policies to encourage small and medium-size industry. But it is a politically sensitive issue and could become more so in the future.

An issue that has become salient more quickly than anyone imagined is that of labor-management relations. The eruption of over 3,000 labor disputes in Korea in the three months following the political changes of June 1987 stunned many observers and aroused a fear that the pent-up demands of labor could not be met without spiraling unrest and economic disorder. The laborers' demands were focused on two areas: wages and the right to form unions other than those sanctioned by existing government regulations. In many instances management found it difficult to respond to these demands because labor, inexperienced in such bargaining, made wage demands beyond the firms' ability to pay and often reopened negotiations after a settlement had been reached.

In late September 1987 it appeared that the pace of labor unrest had slowed. As we have noted, many observers had feared that radical students returning to their campuses would link up with labor, causing the unrest to escalate. But apparently this did not happen, and most of the disputes were being settled within a few days of their outbreak. The early estimates of the economic impact of the labor unrest were alarming, however. With post–June 29 wage increases averaging over 10 percent (total wage increases for January–September 1987 were in the 15 to 20 percent range) and much production lost, the economic forecasts pointed to a 25 percent drop in Korea's trade surplus for 1987, a reduction in GNP growth to 6 percent in the second half of the year, and an additional price increase of 2.6 percent. While there is no doubt that Korea's 1987 economic performance has been seriously affected, it is not yet possible to say how deep or lasting the economic damage will be and how the experience of 1987 will affect labor's demands in the annual spring rounds of wage adjustments in 1988 and beyond.

Labor-management relations are likely to be more complicated and difficult in the future. The extent will depend on whether government, business, and labor move rapidly to build a new framework in which to conduct them. The first task must be to pass new legislation to allow the establishment and recognition of unions and to institute collective bargaining procedures. If such changes are made, Korea is less likely to be criticized in the United States for failing to provide the minimum labor rights called for in the trade bill before the Congress in 1987. Many Koreans of varying political views also told us that the success of new approaches will depend on whether the government can prevent outside agitation and violence in labor disputes.

The nature of the government's role in the economy and the economic policy process is a central issue for the future of Korea. Despite the initial moves toward liberalization, most Korean and American observers doubt that the Korean government will soon or easily relinquish substantial control over the economy. While both government and business representatives attest to some lessening of direct government intervention in business, they also spoke of the heavy dependence of Korean companies on the government for credit and of the government's strong influence over industrial strategy.

In addition, the government may be drawn into the economy in new ways as social and political changes produce a more pluralistic policymaking process in the months and years ahead. Several Koreans told us that whatever the outcome of the upcoming elections, the policy process will be more politicized, and "populist" issues such as social welfare and income distribution will be more important. Some Koreans predicted that one result of this trend would be to make liberalization more difficult, thereby leading to greater friction in U.S.–Korea economic relations.

U.S.–ROK Economic Relations

The economic linkage between the United States and the Republic of Korea is an extremely important and increasingly sensitive part of the overall bilateral relationship. In particular, the rapid increase of Korean exports to the United States and the relatively closed nature of the Korean economy have created strains which threaten to spill over into the political arena.

Over the past five years, Korean exports to the United States have increased at an average annual rate of 20 percent to a level of

$13.3 billion in 1986. Korea, the United States's fourteenth largest trading partner in 1981, had by 1986 moved to seventh place and had become the source of its fifth largest bilateral trade deficit ($7.4 billion). As Korea's number-one export market, the United States took 32 percent of Korea's exports from 1970 to 1985 and 40 percent in 1986. In contrast, U.S. exports to Korea increased at an average annual rate of only 1.5 percent over the past five years—although this record compares favorably with the overall U.S. export performances during the same period. The United States is the second largest source of Korean imports after Japan.

The bilateral trade issue is critical for Korea because its export-led economy is so dependent on the U.S. market and because American pressures on the trade issue have strong domestic political repercussions. For the United States, the issue is not economically critical—its trade deficit with Korea is only 5 percent of its total trade deficit—but it has become highly visible and symbolic in the context of the much more consequential U.S. trade dispute with Japan.

For these reasons the governments and business communities of both countries have been actively seeking ways to address the problem. While defending its need for a modest surplus, Seoul has emphasized preventing further growth of the surplus by restricting somewhat exports to the United States and by promoting imports from the United States. Although American approaches to the dispute are more disparate, they have generally emphasized the opening of Korean markets to American goods and services.

While some progress has been made toward resolving the U.S.–ROK economic differences, much remains to be done. Koreans and Americans still do not agree in their perceptions of the problem and possible solutions to it. Moreover, the need for progress is increasingly urgent as politics in both the United States and Korea creates a growing sense of frustration and impatience.

Korean economic policymakers, politicians, business executives, and scholars share the basic view that Korea is already doing—or committed to doing—enough, if not more than enough, to reduce trade friction. While the policymakers and scholars were more approving of market-opening measures than the politicians and business leaders, all of them argued that because Korea is a small developing country with a short history of economic growth and a per capita income of only $2300, Americans must not expect too much too fast. They emphasized that the Korean current account surplus developed only recently and that it could be reversed. They contended that too rapid an opening of the Korean economy would hurt Korean businesses, especially in the consumer-goods and financial sectors, and would cause a sharp political reaction, especially if it were done in response to U.S. pressures.

We were also told that whatever Korea might do would have little effect on the U.S trade deficit because the U.S. problem is multilateral rather than bilateral. Korean business leaders went on to say that the real reason American business does not do well in the Korean market is not Korean government restraints, but American deficiencies in quality, service, and price. In this they contrasted American performance with that of Japanese companies. They also argued that Japan would continue to benefit more than the United States from Korean market-opening measures because of the advantages Japanese companies enjoy in Korea.

In fact, Korea's economic relationship with Japan bears directly on the U.S.–Korea dispute. Korea has long had a trade deficit with Japan—reaching about $5 billion in 1986—largely because Japan is Korea's principal supplier of capital and intermediate goods, the import of which has risen with Korea's swelling exports. Although the Korean government has recently emphasized shifting import sourcing from Japan to the United States to help reduce the U.S. deficit, almost all the business people we met underscored the difficulty of such a move. They gave several reasons, including the reputation Japanese suppliers enjoy in Korea, the fact that American companies have not been exporting the same goods to Korea, and Japan's geographic proximity and cultural similarity. (In fact, by mid-1987 Korea's trade deficit with Japan seemed to have responded very little if at all to Korean government efforts to diversify imports.)

Finally, all the Koreans with whom we spoke argued against more rapid appreciation of the Korean won against the dollar as a means of lessening the trade deficit. This course has been strongly advocated by the U.S. administration which believes that the won is undervalued. The Koreans pointed out that the won has gained about 10 percent against the dollar since January 1986 and may appreciate further in 1987. The exchange rate is too blunt an instrument for dealing with the U.S.–ROK problem, they said, and would, if used too forcefully, become a political issue very quickly. Moreover, unless the basic causes of the U.S. global trade deficit are effectively addressed, the result would merely be to shift the U.S. deficit from Korea elsewhere.

The arguments presented by Koreans seemed overdrawn on several key points. It is difficult for Americans to appreciate fully the view of many Koreans that their economy is vulnerable and developing when that same economy is very successfully exporting automobiles and consumer electronics into the United States. The Korean plea against U.S. pressure was also undercut by the frank admission of some Korean policymakers and scholars that only U.S. pressure brought about change in Korean policies. The argument for treating the problem as a multilateral issue has to be discounted because Korea depends so heavily on the U.S. market. While Korean policymakers clearly want to avoid repeating the mistakes that helped create the U.S.–Japan trade dispute by advancing these arguments, they risk precisely that.

The perspectives of American business people in Seoul and of American officials differed significantly from those of the Koreans. While the Americans agree that the Korean government is keen to avoid the type of trade frictions now occurring between the United States and Japan, they emphasize that the reality of market opening in Korea falls short of the declared goals. The reasons cited included the preference for governmental control of the economy on the part of bureaucrats and the businesses that benefit from it, the anti-import bias built into the system (import liberalization is carefully planned in consultation with the businesses that will be affected to minimize the impact), and the fear of political repercussions. As we have indicated, the Americans also emphasized that Korean market-opening measures have not been matched by changes in the laws and regulations to permit American companies to compete effectively with Korean companies down to the level of the consumer. As evidence of this, they cited the fact that only 5 percent of American goods imported by Korea are finished products.

We came away from these discussions on the U.S.–Korea economic relationship with the view that while the two sides are not terribly far apart, this is not a time for complacency. Many Koreans and Americans agree broadly that the trade problem is sensitive and urgent, and Korean policymakers are committed at least to policies that lead in the right direction. But each side lacks confidence that the other side truly understands its difficulties. As a result, the Koreans have a tendency to propose partial solutions and to delay the full implementation of the measures adopted by the government. And the Americans are dissatisfied and impatient with what has actually been done. We fear that unless this gap is bridged soon, it will grow wider.

3
Security and
International Relations

*T*he Korean peninsula is critical to regional and global peace and security. Since the Korean War it has been an arena of military confrontation between North and South Korea. With a total of about 1.5 million North Korean and South Korean troops facing each other across the four kilometer–wide DMZ, the possibility of renewed conflict is ever present.

The Korean peninsula is the one location in which the interests of the four major powers—the United States, the Soviet Union, Japan, and the People's Republic of China (PRC)—are directly engaged. The U.S. interest in the security of Korea is reflected in its alliance with the Republic of Korea and in the presence of 40,000 American troops in the South. The Soviet Union and China both have common borders with the Democratic People's Republic of Korea and vie with each other for influence in the North. Chinese troops, of course, fought against United Nations forces during the Korean War. The peninsula, historically a bridge between mainland Asia and the Japanese islands, has always been seen by Japanese as critical to their security, a view which reached its extreme in Japan's colonial occupation of Korea from 1910 to 1945.

The likelihood of war in the Korean peninsula presently seems remote, but the confrontation between North and South continues to pose dangers to peace. All the major powers have demonstrated an active interest in preventing the outbreak of war. The risk of conflict arises mainly from possible future developments in the two Koreas. Some analysts continue to fear that the growing military capability of

South Korea could lead the North to attack while Pyongyang still possesses some military advantage. Many more fear that the North will try to disrupt the Olympics, especially in view of the current impasse in the North-South dialogue. The danger of aggression could be increased by the approaching political transition in the North—as North Korean leader Kim Il Sung seeks to have his son, Kim Jong Il, succeed him—and by political unrest in South Korea which might tempt the North to intervene.

The Division between North and South

The division of Korea had its origins in the conclusion of World War II and the incipient Cold War between the United States and the Soviet Union. American and Soviet forces entered Korea in 1945 to accept the surrender of Japanese troops (the Americans south of the 38th parallel and the Soviets north of it). Over the next three years the two occupying powers failed to establish a unified Korean government and formed separate regimes. The Korean War hardened the division and left the military confrontation between North and South.

Despite the bitterness of the division, reunification of the peninsula remains the proclaimed objective of both Korean governments. But each side seeks the goal on its own terms and by its own means. As a result, the two Koreas, unlike the two Germanys, have had only the most limited contact.

North Korea's isolation and unpredictability add significantly to dangers on the peninsula. Kim Il Sung, the regime's all-powerful leader, has since 1945 laid exclusive claim to the mantle of Korean nationalism and made unification, through force if necessary, the dominant objective of the North Korean state. Short of war, North Korea has constantly sought to destabilize the South Korean government. Most dramatically, North Korean agents attempted in October 1983 to assassinate South Korean President Chun Doo Hwan while he was visiting Rangoon, Burma. Several South Korean officials were killed, including four cabinet members. North Korea's unpredictability also reflects the fact that it is one of the most closed and controlled societies in the world. At least as long as Kim Il Sung is in power, North Korea poses a threat to the South which cannot be dismissed.

The Military Balance   For most of the period since the Korean War, the North has maintained distinct military superiority over the South, posing critical questions about its intentions and necessitating a costly South Korean defense effort. The combination of powerful ROK and U.S. forces and the existence of the U.S.–ROK security alliance have effectively deterred Pyongyang. However, even taking into account the qualitative advantages of the South Korean and U.S. forces, the North still has a quantitative lead in some critical areas, such as number of troops, armor, and artillery. In ground forces, the North enjoys a 200,000-man advantage in personnel (750,000 for the DPRK vs. 542,000 for the ROK/U.S.), a nearly 3:1 advantage in tanks, and a 1.5:1 superiority in artillery. In the air, the quantitative lead enjoyed by the North (680:440 in fighter aircraft) is at least partly offset by the South's far more modern forces. The North Korean navy similarly holds an edge over the ROK navy.

The fact that North Korean forces are deployed offensively heightens the risk of war on the peninsula and the threat to the South. Sixty-five percent of the North's forces, including large numbers of tanks and artillery, are dug in within about 40 miles of the border. North Korea is also believed to have twenty special forces brigades that could be quickly dropped behind ROK lines. As a result, the warning time of an attack on the South could be very short, perhaps as little as 12-24 hours. The danger of this situation for the South lies partly in the fact that one-third of the South's population is within 25–30 miles of the DMZ and that much of its industry is located in Seoul.

Both South Korean and American officials and military officers agree, however, that the military strength of the forces in the South is an adequate deterrent to North Korean attack. The quality of ROK forces—which comprise over 90 percent of total troops in the South—is very high. The U.S. presence provides assurance of a U.S. response in the event of attack. Airpower, including F-16s sold to South Korea in 1981 and five squadrons of U.S. fighter aircraft, would be extremely effective against North Korean forces moving southward. The U.S. role in providing reconnaissance and command, control, and communications facilities is also key to deterrence. U.S. naval support is important to making up the gap in ROK naval capabilities.

Furthermore, the trend in the military balance is moving in favor of the South. All of those with whom we discussed the question agreed on this fact, but there was some disagreement as to when the military capabilities of the South might be roughly equal to those of the North. Some official Korean sources, focusing on quantitative as opposed to qualitative measures, estimated that at present South Korean capabilities are 60 percent of the North's and would, at current rates of growth, reach the 80 percent level in the mid-1990s or toward the end of this century. Other sources thought that the ROK would rival the North in military strength sooner than this.

The main reason for this trend in the military balance is South Korea's more dynamic economy. North Korea has for many years spent a much larger proportion of its GNP on defense than the South: 20–25 percent for the DPRK vs. 5–6 percent for the ROK. But South Korean spending is based on an increasingly larger GNP: $90.5 billion for the South vs. an estimated $18.5 billion for the North in 1986. Thus, in 1986 the absolute amount of South Korean defense expenditure—$5.4 billion—exceeded for the first time North Korean defense expenditure—estimated at $4.6 billion. This gap in defense spending will almost certainly widen in the years ahead given likely GNP growth rates in the South of at least 7-8 percent per year and, in the North, both a stagnant economy and the difficulty of raising further the percentage of GNP directed to the military.

The increasing military strength of South Korea is seen by most South Koreans as providing needed security against attack by the North, but it has also raised questions about the future. One question is whether the present command relationship between ROK and U.S. forces should be changed to reflect the greater ROK contribution. Another question is whether the growing ROK capability should lead to changes in the size and structure of the U.S. forces in Korea. These are subjects to which we shall return below.

Inter-Korean Dialogue   The relationship between the two Koreas has included an on-again, off-again process of dialogue without which there is no hope of eventually reducing tension. As we found in our discussions with South Koreans, distrust is still the dominant element in the relationship. But both sides also have reasons to continue the dialogue.

A major obstacle to North-South dialogue is the actual or perceived divergence in the motivations and approaches of the two sides. The official South Korean view is that the North's true objectives are to weaken the ROK by bringing about the withdrawal of U.S. troops and to unify the peninsula under communism. For this reason the North has consistently preferred high-level talks dealing with political-military affairs and involving the United States ("tripartite talks"). (The Carter administration proposed tripartite talks, but the Reagan administration has set this proposal aside emphasizing instead the bilateral dialogue between North and South.) Failing this, we were told, the North's principal aim has been to affect international and particularly American opinion in the hope that U.S. military forces would be withdrawn, as was their hope at the time of the Carter administration's abortive effort to withdraw U.S. ground forces from the peninsula.

One of the strongest determinants of North Korea's tactics is the political situation in the South. As in early 1986 and mid-1987, Pyongyang has consistently pulled back in some measure from the proposals for dialogue when there has been turmoil in the South.

North Korea's periodic interest in dialogue with the South may in part be an effort to demonstrate to its people that it is serious about reunification. How this calculation will be affected by the political succession process in the North we cannot predict. Pyongyang is also under pressure from China and perhaps the Soviet Union to reduce tension on the peninsula.

What may be more important in the long term is North Korea's need for Western capital and know-how to improve its faltering economy. China has been encouraging North Korea to follow the Chinese example by improving its relations with the West in order to modernize its economy. But so far the North has shown little enthusiasm to act seriously on this advice. Its 1984 joint-venture law has failed to attract Western enterprise, and the DPRK has been declared in default on $770 million in loans provided by Western banks.

South Korea's major objectives in the North-South dialogue are to build confidence between South and North and to create an international framework to safeguard its security before the question of the withdrawal of U.S. forces is addressed. Thus the ROK emphasizes a step-by-step process, focusing initially on economic and humanitarian issues in the bilateral dialogue and on the proposals for United Nations membership and cross-recognition of the two Koreas (described below). The South contends that these issues can and should first be addressed directly by North and South. For these reasons the South has responded with great caution to the North's offer of political-military talks and its insistence on involving the United States.

The government of South Korea is under considerable domestic compulsion to pursue the dialogue. In the South's case, the widespread emotional appeal of unification means that the government cannot be seen as missing meaningful opportunities for contact with the North. Also, in recent years, as its economic and military strength has increased, the South has grown more confident in its approach to North-South relations.

The intermittent North-South dialogue has taken place in three main rounds. The first, in 1972–73, was prompted by the Sino-American rapprochement. It was halted by North Korea, allegedly in response to President Park's tightening of his political control in the South. The second round of dialogue was initiated by Pyongyang in 1979–80 in the wake of President Park's death and included discussion of possible prime ministerial talks, but was broken off by the North after Chun Doo Hwan become ROK president in 1980.

The most recent and active round of North-South dialogue occurred in 1984–85. Seoul's unanticipated acceptance of Pyongyang's offer of aid for flood victims in the South in September 1984 led to three Red Cross talks, a series of economic discussions, two preliminary meetings between ROK and DPRK parliamentarians, and a historic reunion of divided families in September 1985. In January 1986, however, North Korea broke off all of these contacts on the grounds that the annual joint military exercises of U.S. and South Korean forces in February–April 1986 would poison the atmosphere for the talks. Unlike in 1985, when it resumed talks after postponing them for the same reason, the North did not agree to resumption in 1986.

Nevertheless, both sides have continued to put forward proposals and counter-proposals for some sort of talks. North Korea has sought high-level political and military talks involving the two Koreas and the United States if possible. The South has insisted on the resumption of direct Red Cross, economic, and parliamentary talks as a precondition for high-level talks, although it has also suggested a meeting between Chun Doo Hwan and Kim Il Sung. Beginning in early 1987, the ROK also insisted that any talks also include discussion of the possible threat posed to the South by the North's construction of the huge Kumgangsan Dam just north of the DMZ. (South Korean officials have argued that the sudden release of large amounts of water from the dam could flood Seoul and damage its defenses.) More recently, in July 1987, the North proposed deep troop reductions by both sides (including the withdrawal of U.S. troops in the South). The South responded that such talks could only be productive when confidence between North and South is increased. To this end, in summer 1987 South Korea proposed foreign ministerial talks at the U.N. and in September it announced a change of policy to permit—even to encourage—contacts between ROK–DPRK officials.

In the background of the recent efforts at dialogue have been two proposals for stabilizing the situation on the peninsula, both supported by the South and rejected by the North. In 1976 U.S. Secretary of State Henry Kissinger proposed "cross-recognition" of North and South Korea by the major powers; the United States and Japan would recognize North Korea, and the Soviet Union and China would recognize South Korea. A second proposal is that South and North Korea simultaneously become permanent members of the U.N. (both are now permanent observers). North Korea has rejected both ideas as part of a "plot" to perpetuate the division of the peninsula. At a minimum, neither proposal seems likely to be adopted until tensions on the peninsula are further reduced.

The 1988 Olympics   The award to Seoul of the 1988 Olympics has become a critical issue in North-South relations. Although the Olympics are awarded to cities and not to states, South Koreans view the Olympics as conferring international recognition on their extraordinary economic and social progress and as symbolizing their country's coming of age in the modern world, much as the 1964 Olympics did for Japan. South Korea also views the Olympics as a major victory in its rivalry with the North, especially if most or all of the Communist states attend, as now seems likely. By successfully holding the Olympics, the South will not only further enhance its international prestige relative to that of the North, it will strengthen its claim to nationalist legitimacy in the eyes of the Korean people.

For North Korea the prospect of the Olympics being held in Seoul presents a dilemma. On the one hand, the North wants to prevent the South from achieving such a dramatic gain in international recognition, again especially if the Soviet Union, China, and other Communist nations participate. The North Korean regime would certainly find it difficult to explain to its own people why its friends did not fully support it. On the other hand, if some Olympic events were to be held in the North, as has been proposed, Pyongyang would be required to open North Korea to thousands of international visitors. And if they went to Seoul, North Korean athletes would be exposed to the remarkable developments there. Some observers in South Korea fear that the North will seek a way out of its dilemma by mounting terrorist actions that would prevent the Olympics from being held or disrupt them once they are in progress.

In the hope of minimizing this possibility and the risk of a Communist boycott of the games, the International Olympic Committee (IOC) has sought to negotiate some participation by North Korea in the Olympic events. Pyongyang at first proposed that it cohost the Olympics with Seoul and that half of the events *and* of the opening and closing ceremonies take place in the North. After the

IOC rejected this, the North reduced its demand to eight events and justified it in terms of the proportion of the Korean population in the North (one-third). The IOC offered to let the North host four events (two preliminary and two final), and later increased the offer to five. The North has maintained throughout its position on cohosting and other formalities, which the IOC and Seoul have rejected.

The pressure on the North to find some means of participating in the Olympics has been growing as it has seemed more and more likely that both the Soviet Union and China will participate. But by September 17, 1987, a year before the Olympics were to open and the final IOC deadline for sending out invitations to Olympic nations, North Korea had not accepted the IOC offer. Many observers concluded that the North is not really serious about participating in the Olympics. But, though the invitations that went out referred only to Olympics in Seoul, IOC president Juan Antonio Samaranch has said that he would be prepared to reopen the issue of the North's participation at any time.

Korea and the Region

The confrontation between the two Koreas is the focal point—and potentially the flashpoint—of major power relations in Northeast Asia. The policies and actions of South Korea's neighbors—Japan, China, and the Soviet Union—in turn have a major impact on its security. Its relations with these powers, especially Japan and China, are profoundly influenced by a long, complicated, and often difficult history. But the last several years have brought gradual improvements in these relationships which if continued should help to reduce tensions on the peninsula.

Japan Japan's harsh colonial role in Korea created deep animosities between Japanese and Koreans which still inhibit ROK–Japan bilateral relations. In public opinion polls Koreans and Japanese still cite each other as among "least liked" peoples and countries. Koreans resent what they regard as Japanese exploitation and manipulation and frequently accuse Japan of working to keep the peninsula divided. Japanese are regarded as looking down upon Koreans and Korean culture, especially in their treatment of the sizable Korean minority in Japan.

Despite these constraints, Japan's relations with South Korea have developed in constructive, or at least correct, ways in recent years. The most positive steps were the historic visits of Prime Minister Nakasone to Korea in January 1983 and of President Chun to Japan in September 1984. Japan has generally avoided involving itself in and commenting on ROK internal politics, and the ties between the conservative ruling elites in the two countries have been a stabilizing factor. Japanese investment in and trade with South Korea have cut both ways in the relationship. On the one hand, Japanese capital, technology, and management know-how have clearly contributed to Korea's economic success. On the other, as we have noted, Japan's steadily growing trade surplus with Korea has caused considerable friction, although it may be reduced in the future by the appreciation of the yen.

Japanese contacts with the North have also been an irritant in ROK–Japan relations. The left wing of Japan's ruling Liberal Democratic Party and the Japan Socialist Party (JSP) have been in close touch with North Korea and, along with the majority of the Korean community in Japan, have put pressure on the Japanese government to establish formal relations or at least to increase informal dealings with Pyongyang. (The moderate new chairwoman of the JSP, Takako Doi, visited North Korea in September 1987, and carried back to Tokyo a message from DPRK leaders that they hoped for improved relations with Japan under its next prime minister, then about to be chosen.) Japan has had limited trade and other economic contacts with North Korea, although the DPRK's default on Japanese bonds put a damper on these openings in the early 1980s.

While the relationship between South Korea and Japan has improved recently, the United States remains a major factor in the relationship. This is most noticeable in the security area, where the animosity between Japan and Korea caused by the colonial experience has made cooperation virtually impossible. The fact that the United States maintains a security alliance with each country is essential to the security of the other and provides a critical linkage in the regional security system. For instance, American air forces stationed in Japan are now sometimes forward deployed to Korea and would be the first reinforcements to reach Korea in the event of a conflict. Thus any sharp deterioration in U.S.–Japan relations affecting their security ties would threaten Korean security, and any lessening of the U.S. security commitment to either country would strain relations between Korea and Japan.

China China's stance toward the two Koreas has changed significantly since its opening to the West under Deng Xiaoping. Although the PRC maintains its military alliance with North Korea, it seeks most of all to ensure peace on the peninsula. In a difficult balancing act, Beijing also continues to compete with the Soviet Union for influence in Pyongyang while it develops unofficial ties with Seoul. Anxious to develop normal relations with the PRC over the long term, South Korea does not press now for more rapid change. Informal relations between China and South Korea have increased sharply in recent years. Trade between the two countries, much of it direct, reached an estimated level of $1.3 billion in 1986. In 1983 and again in 1985, the PRC and the ROK established direct political contact to deal with a hijacked Chinese airliner, a defecting Chinese airforce pilot, and a Chinese torpedo boat which entered South Korean waters following a mutiny. South Korean companies are actively seeking to invest in China. And China participated in the Asian Games in Seoul in 1986 and seems ready to participate in the Olympics. At the same time the PRC continues to support North Korea's basic stands on unification and North-South dialogue. As it must if it is to maintain its influence in Pyongyang, Beijing endorses the DPRK's demand for tripartite talks and the withdrawal of U.S. troops, though the Chinese understand that such withdrawal is unlikely unless tensions are substantially reduced on the peninsula. China also rejects the calls for cross-recognition and simultaneous U.N. membership of the two Koreas. However, China has sought gently to prod and entice the

North into dialogue with the South and to persuade the United States to be more open to the North. In the spring of 1987, for instance, the PRC conveyed to the DPRK a new American proposal offering the North modestly expanded contacts with the United States if the North agreed to resume its dialogue with the South and to participate in the Olympics (we are not aware of any North Korean response). Kim Il Sung's visit to Beijing in May 1987 provided China an opportunity to press these points.

The Soviet Union The relationship between the Soviet Union and North Korea goes back to the central Soviet role in establishing the North Korean state and installing Kim Il Sung as its leader. Although Kim Il Sung has very successfully played the Soviets off against the Chinese and the Soviet–DPRK relationship has had its ups and downs, Soviet support for North Korea has been and remains a critical factor in the Korean situation.

The period since 1984 has been one of closer relations between Moscow and Pyongyang. Kim Il Sung visited Moscow in 1984 and in late 1986 for discussions that were useful but did not produce agreement on all issues. The Soviets have agreed to provide increased economic and military aid, including a squadron of MiG-23 fighter aircraft, a step that would not shift the basic military balance on the peninsula. In exchange the North Koreans have granted overflight rights for Soviet reconnaissance aircraft traveling to Vietnam along the Chinese coast, thus facilitating reconnaissance, and have allowed ceremonial port visits by Soviet naval vessels. One joint air exercise has been reported. So far, however, the actual extent of military cooperation seems more symbolic than real.

Most observers agree that the Soviet Union does not want war on the peninsula. This would seem to be truer than ever following Soviet leader Mikhail Gorbachev's announcement in a speech in Vladivostok in July 1986 that the Soviet Union intends to develop more positive relations in Northeast Asia.

The United States and Korean Security

The most important aspect of American policy toward the Korean peninsula is the U.S. commitment to the security of South Korea. That commitment is embodied in the American military presence in South Korea and demonstrated by regular military exercises that also involve external U.S. naval, air, and land forces.

While the U.S. military presence is widely supported by Koreans, new realities on the peninsula—the growing capability of the ROK military, domestic political change, and greater national pride and sensitivity among Koreans—have raised several issues concerning the future character of the U.S. military presence.

The most important—but not urgent—of these issues is how the U.S. security commitment to Korea will continue to be demonstrated through the U.S. military presence. It was suggested to us that as the ROK military capability improves, the key to any possible future changes in the composition of U.S. forces in Korea would be to maximize the complementarity and reduce the duplication of U.S. and ROK military capabilities without weakening deterrence.

A second issue concerning the future U.S. military role in Korea is the command relationships between the U.S. and Korean military. At present a U.S. four-star general is commander-in-chief (CINC) of the Combined Forces Command (CFC) which would include, in wartime, all U.S. and Korean forces. In addition to command of the combined forces, the U.S. general has command of the United Nations Command (in fulfillment of U.S. responsibilities to maintain the armistice) and of the United States Forces in Korea.

We found that the present command structure is being questioned for two reasons. First, the growing capability of the ROK forces, including their increased professionalism, has led to dissatisfaction with the Korean role in the combined command structure. Second, a perception exists in Korea that under the current command structure the U.S. commander of the CFC has complete control over all U.S. and Korean forces on a day-to-day basis and that, therefore, any actions by ROK forces are subject to the control of the U.S. commander.

With regard to the ROK role in the Combined Forces Command, many Koreans and Americans now feel that a Korean officer should command the combined *ground* forces because the ROK army provides, as we have noted, more than 90 percent of these forces. We understand that such a change is already under preliminary discussion between the ROK and U.S. defense departments. Assigning more of the ground forces in Korea to that command would underscore the military role of the forces and their commanders. At present, some key Korean as well as American units are not assigned to the CFC in peacetime.

Korean perceptions of the relationship between the U.S. commander and the ROK forces are a complex matter. Under the 1978 agreement between the United States and Korea, the U.S. commander has operational control of all forces assigned to him by the U.S. and ROK defense establishments. However, as noted, neither the U.S. nor the ROK assigns all their forces in Korea to the CFC in peacetime. And even for those that are assigned, both nations reserve the right to withdraw units from the command when their individual national interests demand such action. Thus, barring a defense emergency, if the ROK wishes to use units assigned to the CFC for domestic purposes, and makes proper notification, the CINC CFC cannot prevent the ROK from using the forces for such actions.

A lack of understanding of existing command arrangements has caused many Koreans, especially students, to accuse the United States of complicity when ROK forces have been used in the past to suppress violent protest which could not be contained by the Korean police. In particular, the 1980 Kwangju incident has left a bitter and confused legacy. In that incident, Korean forces were sent to the southwestern city of Kwangju to quell disorder following the imposition of martial law. None of the ROK forces involved in the large number of casualties early in the incident were under U.N. command, and the United States was not aware of their deployment. Subsequently, different ROK forces experienced in civil control were withdrawn from the CFC and sent to Kwangju to restore governmental authority and did so with a minimum of casualties. The ROK used proper notification procedures in withdrawing these forces.

Nonetheless, because of the emotion surrounding that incident, the misperception of U.S. responsibility has never been successfully corrected. This misperception has been played upon not only by North Korea, but also by certain elements in South Korea in their opposition to the Chun government and to American support for it. It has, many Koreans told us, quite widely influenced Korean attitudes toward the overall U.S.–Korea relationship, especially among students.

A third issue regarding the U.S. military presence in Korea has to do with the sizable number of American military at the CFC/U.S. forces headquarters in downtown Seoul. Although this location dates from the Korean War period, it is becoming more visible and potentially a greater source of irritation and embarrassment to Koreans as space in Seoul grows scarcer and the city becomes more international.

We concluded from our discussions of the issues surrounding the U.S. military presence that they are among the most sensitive facing the United States in Korea and that they deserve careful attention from American opinion leaders and policymakers. Most of those with whom we discussed these issues agreed that no change should be made in the command relationships or in the composition of U.S. forces before the 1988 Olympics for fear of sending the wrong signal to North Korea. But most agreed that some changes would be appropriate after 1988.

On the matter of U.S. policy toward North Korea and the North-South dialogue, we detected little if any concern among the Koreans with whom we spoke. In general, the United States shares the South Korean view that the problem of reunification must be worked out by the two Korean sides. While skeptical of North Korean intentions, the United States believes that a dialogue between South and North is necessary and supports the South's "gradual approach" and its focus on economic and humanitarian issues as a way of building confidence. As already mentioned, the present U.S. administration has not favored tripartite talks and has indicated that if an expanded forum were appropriate, it would share the South Korean preference for quadripartite talks involving South Korea, North Korea, China, and the United States. South Korean flexibility on this issue may increase in the future. In any event, the United States sees the need for the Soviet Union to be engaged in efforts to reduce tensions on the peninsula. Finally, the United States supports the South Korean desire for simultaneous membership of both countries in the U.N. and for eventual cross-recognition of the two Koreas.

In general, American policy is not to negotiate with North Korea in any forum. But in April 1987, the United States announced a change in its policy on contacts between American and North Korean diplomats. In the interest of reducing tensions on the peninsula and facilitating North-South dialogue and a successful 1988 Olympics, the United States now allows American diplomats to discuss concrete matters with North Korean diplomats at social events or in neutral (non-bilateral) settings. This change was discussed in advance with the ROK government, which concurred in it.

4
Korea's Future: Implications for American Policy

G iven its security and economic interests in Korea, the United States has a large stake in Korean political progress and should pursue policies to actively promote it. But as Americans look to the future and consider their policy options, it is important to understand that Korea is not a second Philippines, on the brink of collapse or revolution. Nor is it a second Japan, a giant, economically and politically able to withstand repeated bouts of bashing from the United States. Respectful, forthright dealings will be essential if the strains and rancor that have developed in U.S.–Japan trade relations are to be avoided.

In the short term, before the presidential elections, American behavior could be of considerable significance. Koreans are proud of their achievements and do not fear—indeed they welcome—the prospect of demonstrating them to the world. Nonetheless, Korea's democratic enterprise is still fragile. Heavy-handed or careless actions and statements by Americans could easily get swept up in the heat of the campaign.

In the longer run, while there is reason to be hopeful, it is by no means assured that Korea will be successful in negotiating the crossroads at which it now stands. Therefore, perhaps more than in most places, the United States needs to pursue careful and well-coordinated policies that are reasonable and clearly defined and that are implemented with due sensitivity. The United States must also proceed with a full understanding of the nature and extent of our influence over domestic Korean events, a point to which we return at the end of this report.

Economic Issues

Economic issues will continue to be a critical component of the U.S.–Korea relationship, and U.S. policy in this area must focus on improving and expanding access to the Korean market. We did not try to identify specific areas of the ROK economy for further liberalization, although as a general matter we believe the services sector merits such treatment. Much has already been achieved. Korean planners have committed themselves to a general policy of opening up markets and have identified areas for priority attention. In addition, won appreciation, currently a high-priority U.S. interest, is likely to continue even though Korean officials argue publicly against it. (U.S. policymakers may, however, find that the rapid rate of appreciation previously sought is now economically less justified as a result of large wage increases and decreased competitiveness of Korean exports.)

What we are most concerned about in the economic relationship is that, even after areas of legitimate concern have been identified, Korean officials either are not prepared, or at least are not able, to peel away all the layers obstructing the efforts of U.S. firms to actually market their products. Korea has earned a reputation for bargaining hard but for honestly implementing any agreements reached. That reputation is being threatened as some American business executives, particularly those dealing in consumer products, think they have solved market-access problems only to find that a myriad of licensing and other legal and regulatory obstacles constrain actual transactions.

A key part of economic relations is the issue of national treatment, i.e., treating foreign interests or businesses on an equal footing with domestic firms. The United States offers national treatment to foreign companies; in only a few areas such as commercial banking, does Korea also. It seems only reasonable that more American firms abroad, including those in Korea, begin to receive such treatment on a reasonable liberalization schedule.

Regardless of how much individual U.S. firms may benefit, we have no illusions that market-opening measures will dramatically affect the bilateral trade balance or the overall U.S. balance of payments. The principal causes of America's trade deficit lie in U.S. domestic policies. In addition, as we have said, the newly found voice of Korean labor may reduce Korea's competitiveness in some areas, and pressures will build in Korea to slow certain aspects of economic liberalization. Negotiations may become more difficult in light of the critical role Korea's economic performance has played in maintaining political stability and given the greater "pluralism" likely to develop in economic policymaking. As Korea passes through this transitional stage, frustrated Americans will need to keep in mind that hurting the Korean economy is counter to U.S. interests. Big sticks should not be used over small issues.

Moreover, during the two months before the election, we recommend that no new cases be instituted for relief against unfair trade practices under Section 301 of the Trade Act of 1974. We are keenly aware of the potential problem this poses for the Reagan administration as it seeks to fend off the worst provisions of the trade bill now pending before Congress. But given the interrelationship between politics and economics in Korea, we believe severe new economic pressure in this period could set back both democratization and the prospects for continuing economic liberalization.

Despite these reasons for sensitivity both before and after the election, and however small and tentative many Koreans consider their economic success to be, the confidence of the principal economic officials in Seoul tallies more with our own sense of an important economic power on the rise. Furthermore, just as the United States cannot ignore Korea's political and economic realities, Koreans cannot ignore ours. Occasional, well-focused pressure may be necessary to make the point. Korean failure to open their market at a reasonable pace and in meaningful ways (i.e., without providing "solutions" that merely cloak further layers of obstruction) will inflict considerable damage on U.S. efforts to maintain the relatively free trading system so crucial to both countries and will lead to onerous trade actions against Korea.

No less than with other trading partners, our relationship must be based on broadly conceived mutual interest, carried out in concrete cases with sensitivity, sincerity, and mutual respect. Anything less on either side will lead us along a very troubled course as our economic interdependence grows.

Security and International Relations

Security relations between the United States and Korea are generally sound. But as we have noted, there is an evolution taking place in both attitudes and actual military strength. Based on our examination of these issues, we believe it is inevitable and healthy that adjustments be made in the command structure.

For the reasons already explained, it would be difficult and unhelpful to try to name a Korean to replace the American who is United Nations (and simultaneously Combined Forces) Commander. As long as the United States, as U.N. Commander, is responsible for maintenance of the armistice agreement, and as long as there is such heavy reliance on U.S. air and naval power for defense of South Korea, the present arrangement at the top is sensible and probably necessary.

But given the disparity in ground-force levels between the ROK and the United States, assigning peacetime command of that component to a Korean would be appropriate. (As in Europe, different command arrangements might be required in case of war.) This step would have the political benefit of giving due recognition to Korean national pride and encouragement to its professionalism. It might also help reduce some of the confusion over the fact that, ultimately, Seoul can dispose of its forces as it sees fit, even for domestic purposes. The United States may never fully convince most Koreans that such is the case, but the change could help at least marginally.

The high visibility of headquarters elements in Seoul, which we noted earlier as a likely source of growing irritation, also deserves further examination. It has been only a minor problem to date, but in a context of rising nationalism, some of which is pointed directly at the U.S. military role, we believe it is timely to face the issue now, before it becomes more contentious.

Over a longer period of time, as indicated, the two governments may want to consider reconfiguring U.S. forces in Korea to take greater account of growing South Korean strength in some areas, while recognizing the continuing need for U.S. complementary support in others. Projections indicate a particular role for the United States in air and naval defense and in command, control, communications, and intelligence (including early warning). Full coordination between the ROK and the United States will be necessary in considering any adjustments, and it will be essential to assure effective deterrence against North Korea through maintenance of the unambiguous U.S. commitment to defense of the ROK in a way that ensures automatic involvement of American forces.

Other defense-related issues that may become problematic include the further development of the ROK defense industry. Though depressed recently, Korean arms exports are already large. They may become even more attractive as a source of employment and foreign exchange earnings, but will aggravate existing tensions in U.S. technology transfer and competition for sales in Korea and third country markets. Depending on potential purchasers, arms sales will carry foreign policy implications as well. These problems could impinge on U.S. arms sales to the ROK as well as on commercial trade.

Problems could also develop with respect to any future regional role in Asia for U.S. forces stationed on the peninsula. Today those forces concentrate solely on defending the ROK. Some people favor expanding their mission over time to be part of a larger Pacific strategy designed primarily to counter the USSR. Such a role might prove attractive to a regional military commander, but it would pose serious questions for U.S.–ROK relations and for overall U.S. national security strategy in Asia and the Pacific. Decisions with respect to this issue would have to be taken in light of Seoul-Pyongyang relations, as well as the general state of U.S.–Soviet relations and Soviet military activity in the region and factors relating to China and Japan.

Despite the high propaganda component of the proposals made by both sides, we believe the South has handled its relations with the North in a reasonable manner. Their step-by-step, confidence-building approach is sensible. So, too, is the U.S. government's stance of not getting ahead of the ROK by independent overtures to the DPRK. America should not abet Pyongyang's efforts to split Seoul and Washington and to bring about an untimely U.S. troop withdrawal. We understand the Seoul government's reluctance to risk interference from Pyongyang by getting too deeply engaged in dialogue with the North at a time of delicate political transition in the South. At the same time, the United States should discuss frankly with the ROK the American national interest in reducing tensions on the peninsula and in having both Seoul and Washington pursue policies that foster the North-South dialogue. Whether the issue is direct contact or trade with the North, military exercises, visa policy, or the number of parties sitting at the negotiating table, the American objectives remain strengthening the prosperity and security of the South and reducing tensions throughout Korea and the region.

Principal responsibility for the confrontation lies, of course, with the DPRK, and without a more realistic and forthcoming approach from Pyongyang, little progress can be expected. Nonetheless, the tentative exchanges in 1984–85 give some reason to believe that there are people in North Korea who see their best hope in a degree of reconciliation with Seoul. Thus, as the South Korean domestic situation settles down, Seoul should devote renewed efforts to revitalizing the North-South dialogue. In the meantime, while no one in or out of Korea should naïvely dismiss the threat from the North, by "crying wolf" so often, the government has, as we suggested earlier, led disaffected students and other younger Koreans to feel that the "threat" is merely a pretext for domestic repression. We believe there is a real threat; by exaggerating and misusing it on frequent occasions, the Korean government has reduced security rather than enhanced it by convincing many of its own citizens otherwise.

Measures that strengthen ROK relations with China or the Soviet Union are also desirable, and they might ultimately contribute to successful entry of both Korean delegations to the United Nations and to cross-recognition, which we favor. Again, however, any real prospects in these areas will depend very heavily on North Korean attitudes. The U.S. responsibility will be to work within the existing range of possibilities to promote ties and reduce mistrust. We should hold no illusions that our role can be more than marginal under present circumstances.

Korean-Japanese relations have a special history and a special sensitivity, but despite lingering bitterness, those relations are critical to maintenance of stability in the region. To some extent the United States can be a buffer, for example as the conduit through which most security cooperation takes place. Increasingly, however, the reality of mutual dependence across the whole range of economic, political, and security issues will have to overcome the legacy of antagonism. The gestures made through exchanges of leadership visits in recent years are a good base on which to build a positive, if still competitive, relationship. Soviet charges of a U.S.–Japan-Korea alliance grossly distort the reality. But the fact is that cooperative ties across the board between South Korea and Japan are of great importance to U.S. interests in the region. Such ties threaten no one, while their absence would contribute to regional instability and weakened deterrence against military adventurism.

Politics

Having conducted our study through a period of high drama running from stalemate to repression, confrontation, and accommodation, we have emerged hopeful but concerned about the future of Korean politics. Both the government and the opposition contributed to the stalemate leading to Chun's April 13 decision, and some elements in both camps continue to adopt confrontational attitudes. Moreover, as we have said, especially at the height of the labor disputes but for reasons going beyond them, we heard frequently that the next Korean government cannot go two years without a major crisis.

Nonetheless, we believe that because the decisions taken since June 29 are consistent with the aspirations of the Korean people, they are far more likely to succeed than previous outmoded and unpopular patterns of governance.

The Korean people have new hope—and expectations—that their leaders will act responsibly and with vision, putting into practice their statesmanlike rhetoric about placing the nation's well-being above personal ambition. They will, as one thoughtful Korean put it, need to differentiate politics from right and wrong, to inculcate in people how to operate in a democracy, how to compromise.

Demonstrably free and fair elections will be crucial to maintaining momentum, though, even with the inevitable horde of foreign observers, such judgments must be made by the Korean people applying Korean criteria. If the procedures are generally accepted, then democracy requires that everyone, including the losers, accept the results of the election. If the political leadership can set a pattern of dialogue and compromise and adherence to democratically established rules, this will serve as a model for others such as labor and management as they seek to resolve their differences.

Drawing a distinction between tolerance of sharply different views and tolerance of disruptive action would also contribute to popular understanding of the proper limits of democracy. We believe it is essential for parties and individual leaders to take unequivocal stands against violence and destructive activities from whatever source, but we agree with those Koreans who think that their country is strong enough to sustain debate across a broader political spectrum and that it has more to gain from reducing alienation of people on the extremes than in shutting them out.

The political landscape of Korea has shifted, and whatever happens in the future, we do not expect to see a return to the previous situation. The demand for democracy will persist. Frequently caught between the veto power of the army and that of the students, the people clearly want neither military intervention nor revolution. In this context, we believe it essential that leaders in all camps avoid another cycle of upheaval and reaction and that they use this election as a launching pad for legitimate, democratic government.

A key factor sometimes overlooked outside Korea, with our focus on the election, is the role of President Chun Doo Hwan. There is no question he was unenthusiastic about changing the constitution in the first place, that he was essentially forced by events to accept some of the June 29 measures such as restoring rights to Kim Dae Jung, and that he is wary about the possibility of an opposition victory. Yet the fact is that he accepted these things. And we take at face value his protestations that he does not seek to perpetuate himself in power from behind the scenes after leaving office and that he does not give priority to short-term political considerations over the positive judgment he hopes history will render on his presidency.

At the same time, there is no reason to believe he has changed his views about the importance of stability and order as an underpinning of security and prosperity. On the contrary, he has continued to make that point. As he faces the end of his tenure, he is likely to be even more sensitive to actions that seem to challenge his legacy of a peaceful transfer of power. The more that people make reasonable efforts to accommodate this reality, and the clearer Chun can foresee a secure future in which he can play an appropriate "senior statesman" role, the greater will be the chances that Korea will awaken on February 25, 1988 to inaugurate a new president and a new era. Otherwise we fear the odds of yet another military crackdown will rise. Rather than the "cleansing" effect some would see in military intervention, we believe the result would be a tragic polarization of Korea.

The American Role

The United States has been inconsistent over the years in the level of public attention it has given to Korean politics, but the judgment of a number of Koreans that the United States is a friend of dictatorship and not of the people is unfair. It is a fact that the United States has worked with authoritarian regimes in Seoul and, at times, has demonstrated a degree of rapport with them that is offensive to Korean perceptions. But the United States has had to deal with a very real threat from North Korea and a continuing need to maintain ROK security. In addition, the blame leveled at the United States for the tragedy at Kwangju—which stems from erroneous assumptions about American control over Korean forces—is also unjust.

In part the perception of American indifference to political reform is due to the reality that, as in so many other places where Washington's interests are importantly engaged, those interests have often outstripped U.S. leverage. The two levers often cited—trade sanctions and troop withdrawals—would inflict far more harm on American interests than any conceivable gain.

The United States does have influence, in part simply because people think it does. One should not underestimate the importance of the U.S. factor in the legitimation of any Korean regime. That influence was exercised, among other times, in 1980–81 to save Kim Dae Jung's life and in 1985 to help kill the repressive Campus Stabilization Law. The example of American support for democracy in the Philippines may even have influenced Chun Doo Hwan's decision of April 30, 1986 to allow debate on constitutional revision.

We should recognize, however, that the attempt to exert influence in Korea can create deep—and sometimes lasting—resentments. This is not a reason to desist from taking a position when the issue is important, but Korean pride must be kept in mind when we assess in advance the effects of our interventions. For example, Americans who go to Korea to observe the elections should eschew any role as "investigating teams." They should be sensitive to the resentment virtually all Koreans would feel toward the type of intrusive role that was so crucial in the very different situation in the Philippines in February 1986.

On February 6, 1987, Assistant Secretary of State Gaston Sigur gave a speech—subsequently endorsed in Seoul by Secretary of State George Shultz—that skillfully set publicly articulated U.S. policy on the fine line between interference and respectful advice. Giving full recognition to Korea's security requirements, Sigur called for a more open and legitimate political system that is creative, responsive, and capable of building consensus through discussion and compromise. Workers' rights must be protected, he said. Politics must be permanently "civilianized." The system must be open and fair. Addressing the sensitive issue of how to treat a retired president, Sigur called for courage, self-sacrifice, and statesmanship. He tempered his speech by saying that political transition should proceed at a pace consistent with harmony and stability. But, he persisted, "Koreans want change." In line with this approach, as tension built during the spring, the United States made plain its opposition to martial law or other forms of military intervention in the political process.

Opposition figures and DJP members alike told us the most important thing the United States could do in the coming election period—in addition to remaining neutral among candidates—was to continue our firm support for democratization and our opposition to military intervention. We fully endorse those points and are confident they represent U.S. policy. Nonetheless, we would underscore that Korea is now in a very delicate period, and Koreans will be listening for the slightest nuance in American policy that can be used—or misused—in some way. It will be essential that the official American voice be precise and firm and that it be consistent in all its manifestations.

In the end, of course, it will be up to Koreans to display the restraint and imagination needed to forestall the showdown many fear. Koreans must understand, however, that any disruption of political progress—particularly from extreme street violence or a military coup—would elicit a strong American reaction.

A series of events in 1987 and 1988 will focus attention back on Korea: the campaign in November, the presidential election in December, inauguration in February, National Assembly elections in April, and the Olympics in September. Throughout, Americans will need to remind ourselves that what counts is not our preferences or judgments, but those of the Korean people. We will also need to keep in mind that these steps are but the beginning of a long and difficult process in a country that will continue to grow in importance for the United States. As the ROK moves ahead with democratization, opens its economy, and strengthens its security, relations with the United States will mature and, in that process, become more complicated. If handled well on both sides, however, those relations should continue to prosper.